P9-CQG-071

THE LIFE CYCLE OF A

DAISY

By L. L. Owens

Published by The Child's World®
1980 Lookout Drive
Mankato, MN 56003-1705
800-599-READ
www.childsworld.com

The Child's World®: Mary Berendes, Publishing Director
The Design Lab: Kathleen Petelinsek, design
Red Line Editorial: Editorial direction

Photographs ©: Harkamal Nijjar/iStockphoto, cover, (top left),
1 (top left); iStockphoto, cover (top right, bottom left, bottom
right), 1 (top right, bottom left, bottom right), 3, 17, 31 (bottom);
Shutterstock Images, 5, 6, 10; Andrei Dumitru/Shutterstock
Images, 9, 31 (top); Steve Gschmeissner/Science Photo Library/
Photo Researchers, Inc., 13, 30 (middle); Jim Pruitt/iStockphoto,
14, 30 (bottom); Bochkarev Photography/iStockphoto, 18,
31 (middle); Fernando Alonso Herrero/iStockphoto, 21; Sonja
Garnitschnig/iStockphoto, 22, 30 (top); Robert Morton/
iStockphoto, 25; Ruta Saulyte-Laurinaviciene/iStockphoto, 26;
Jason Verschoor/iStockphoto, 29

ISBN: 978-1-60973-146-5
LCCN: 2011927734

Printed in the United States of America
Mankato, MN
July 2011
PA02089

TABLE OF CONTENTS

LIFE CYCLES

Every living thing has a life cycle. A life cycle is the steps a living thing goes through as it grows and changes. Humans have a life cycle. Animals have a life cycle. Plants have a life cycle, too.

A cycle is something that happens over and over again. A life cycle begins with the start of a new life. It continues as a plant or creature grows. And it keeps going as one living thing creates another, or **reproduces**—and the cycle starts over again.

A daisy's life cycle has several steps: from seed it grows into a mature daisy.

Like a butterfly, a daisy has a life cycle.

At the center of a daisy are many **disk flowers**.

DAISIES

A daisy is a plant that makes flowers. There are many kinds of flowering plants on Earth. They are found in most places—from mountain meadows to sandy deserts.

Daisy flowers grow on long stalks. The stalks of an oxeye daisy are 2 feet (60 cm) tall. Most daisy plants have long leaves with an oval shape. Each leaf has a jagged edge.

Each flower head has a button, or disk, in the center. On the disk are many tiny tube-shaped flowers. They are called disk flowers.

Surrounding the disk are long plant parts often called petals. They are actually flowers, too, called **ray flowers**. They can be many colors.

Daisies grow best in rich soil, full of minerals and nutrients. Like most plants, daisies cannot sit in soggy ground for too long. In soggy soil, less oxygen can reach plants.

Daisies thrive with plenty of fresh water and bright sunshine. But they can stay healthy even with poor soil and some shade. Summer is when daisy flowers are in full bloom.

Daisies thrive in the sunshine.

Daisy seeds grow from the head of the flower.

SPROUTING

Daisies grow from seeds. The hard shell of a daisy seed protects its contents. Inside a seed is an **embryo** and its food. An embryo is a plant that has not sprouted. Around the embryo is food it needs to stay alive during cold months. Birds and other animals like to eat seeds for the food inside. If daisy seeds survive the winter, they will sprout in spring.

When a seed **germinates**, t begins to sprout. For Shasta daisy seeds to germinate, the temperature has to be just right—between 65 and 70 degrees Fahrenheit.

Sprouting occurs around late spring to summer. First, the seed absorbs water from the soil. Then it swells and the seed shell splits open.

By now, the first tiny root is growing down from the seed. It works its way deeper into the soil to find a good water source. When it finds a good spot, the root grows. More roots grow and spread out in the soil. These roots hold the plant in the ground. They also absorb water and nutrients from the soil. Tiny hair-like threads grow from the roots.

With special tools, people can see what daisy seeds look like up close.

Daisy seedlings have two leaves called **cotyledons**.

A NEW DAISY

Soon, a daisy sprout pushes its way to the soil's surface. Two small green leaves on one stem poke out of the ground. These early leaves are called cotyledons. They act as a food source for the sprout.

The daisy begins making food using sunlight through **photosynthesis**. The cotyledons trap the sunlight to produce the food they need to grow. Other creatures, such as insects, eat the cotyledons. These **herbivores** get energy from the food stored in the leaves.

As the plant grows, new leaves grow from its stems. It is now a seedling. The young daisy's stems and leaves work hard to help it survive. The stems take water from the roots and move it up through the plant. The leaves absorb sunlight to make food. And the plant will later store its food in its seeds and flower nectar.

Young daisy plants have many roots that find nutrients in the soil.

A daisy bud opens to reveal the many flowers on a daisy head.

As spring goes on, the daisy keeps growing taller. It becomes a mature daisy and is able to reproduce. By summer, the plant grows bucs and is ready to bloom. The buds are kept safe from bugs and the weather by sepals. These are plant parts that cover the buds.

When the plant is ready, the buds open to reveal flowers. Each flower head is mcde of many, many flowers. Daisies continue to bloom into the fall. Insects and diseases don't usually bother daisies. They are able to produce many blossoms.

MAKING SEEDS

A mature daisy can reproduce, or create new daisies. Each disk or ray flower has both male and female parts inside. Pistils are a flower's female **reproductive** parts. They are located in the center of each disk flower. Thread-like stamens surround each pistil. Stamens are the male reproductive parts. A stamen creates pollen, a sticky powder containing male cells.

For the daisy, reproduction depends on **pollination**. Pollination is an important part of the life cycle for most plants. For pollination to happen, the pollen needs to get from a daisy's stamen to a pistil.

Many pistils and stamens are at the center of a daisy.

Pollen collects on a bee's legs as it drinks nectar from a daisy.

Pollen may be carried to the pistil by bees or butterflies. These and other animals visit a daisy flower looking for nectar. This is the sweet liquid that daisies make to attract insects. While an insect drinks nectar, pollen sticks to its legs or body. The pollen lands on the tip of the pistil, where it can **fertilize** the egg inside.

After pollination occurs, daisy seeds form at the base of the pistil. One daisy flower can make hundreds of seeds. Blooms die off and the seeds fall to the ground. Seeds may scatter in the wind. They may be buried by a squirrel or other animal. Or maybe a gardener will collect the seeds for planting.

Blooms die off and seeds form after daisies are pollinated.

When winter comes, daisy plants lose their leaves.

Seeds come in their own hard shell. They can survive being moved around. But many end up in places where they cannot grow. A few end up in a good spot in the soil. A daisy's parent plant loses all of its leaves when winter comes. In cold places, some daisies die during the winter. Other daisy plants just stop making leaves. They wait until spring to grow again.

Seeds wait months through the cold weather. In spring, the seeds start to grow. Each seed's embryo develops. Water and warmth help the newly formed roots take hold underground. Early sprouts appear above ground. Flowers may appear that first year. But some kinds of daisies take two years to grow flowers. When they do, pollination occurs and new seeds grow. The life cycle of the daisy continues.

Each spring, new daisies grow from seeds that survived the winter.

D A I S Y

LIFE CYCLE DIAGRAM

Pollination

Seed

Cotyledon

30

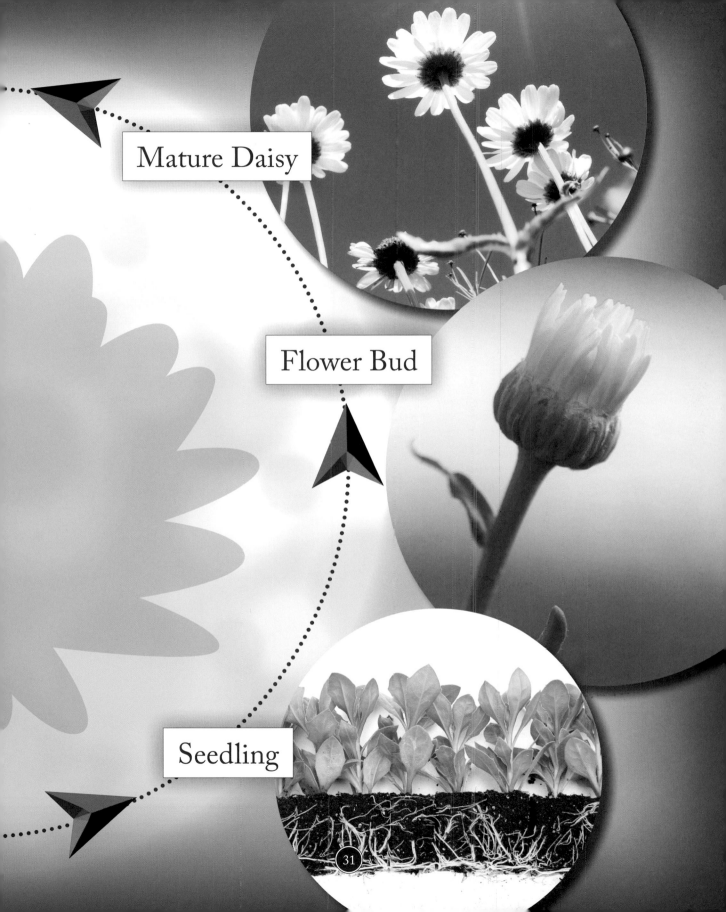

Mature Daisy

Flower Bud

Seedling

Web Sites

Visit our Web site for links about the life cycle of a daisy: **childsworld.com/links**

Note to Parents, Teachers, and Librarians: We routinely verify our Web links to make sure they are safe and active sites. So encourage your readers to check them out!

Books

Aloian, Molly, and Bobbie Kalman. *The Life Cycle of a Flower*. New York: Crabtree Publishing, 2004.
Carle, Eric. *The Tiny Seed*. New York: Little Simon, 2009
Huseby, Victoria. *Daisy*. Mankato, MN: Smart Apple Media, 2009.

Glossary

cotyledons (kot-l-EED-nz): Cotyledons are the first leaves of a plant. From daisy seeds grow cotyledons.

disk flowers (DISK FLOU-urz): Disk flowers are the tiny flowers at the center of a daisy bloom. The center of a daisy flower has many disk flowers.

embryo (EM-bree-oh): An embryo is an organism in the early stages of growth. Inside a daisy seed is an embryo.

fertilize (FUR-tuh-lize): To fertilize is when a male reproductive cell joins a female reproductive cell to create a new life. Insects help fertilize daisies.

germinates (JUR-muh-nates): When a seed germinates, it begins growing roots and shoots. In spring, a daisy seed germinates.

herbivores (HUR-buh-vors): Herbivores are animals that eat plants, not other animals. Some herbivores like to eat cotyledons.

photosynthesis (foh-toh-SIN-thuh-siss): Photosynthesis is a process within green plants that changes light energy into food energy. Daisies make food through photosynthesis.

pollination (POL-uh-na-shun): Pollination is the process of moving pollen from a stamen to a pistil, resulting in fertilization. Bees and other insects are needed for daisy pollination.

ray flowers (RAY FLOU-urz): Ray flowers are the petals that surround a head of disk flowers. Each daisy petal is a ray flower.

reproduces (ree-pruh-DOOS-ez): If an animal or plant reproduces, it produces offspring. A daisy reproduces to make new daisies.

reproductive (ree-pruh-DUCK-tiv): A reproductive cell or body part is used in making new creatures. Each daisy flower has both female and male reproductive parts.

Index